PETER RABBIT™

MAD LIBS  JUNIOR

by Sarah Fabiny

Mad Libs

An Imprint of Penguin Random House

MAD LIBS
Penguin Young Readers Group
An Imprint of Penguin Random House LLC

Mad Libs format copyright © 2018 by Penguin Random House LLC. All rights reserved.

Concept created by Roger Price & Leonard Stern

Published by Mad Libs,
an imprint of Penguin Random House LLC,
345 Hudson Street, New York, New York 10014.
Printed in the USA.

ISBN 9780241336380
1 3 5 7 9 10 8 6 4 2

MAD LIBS ☺ JUNIOR.
INSTRUCTIONS

MAD LIBS JUNIOR® is a game for kids who don't like games!
It can be played by one, two, three, four, or forty.

RIDICULOUSLY SIMPLE DIRECTIONS:

At the top of each page in this book, you will find four columns of words, each headed by a symbol. Each symbol represents a part of speech. The symbols are:

★	☺	➡	?
NOUNS	**ADJECTIVES**	**VERBS**	**MISC.**

MAD LIBS JUNIOR® is fun to play with friends, but you can also play it by yourself! To begin, look at the story on the page below. When you come to a blank space in the story, look at the symbol that appears underneath. Then find the same symbol on this page and pick a word that appears below the symbol. Put that word in the blank space, and cross out the word, so you don't use it again. Continue doing this throughout the story until you've filled in all the spaces. Finally, read your story aloud and laugh!

EXAMPLE:

"Goodbye!" he said, as he jumped into his _____ and _____
    ★   ➡

off with his pet _____.
    ?

★	☺	➡	?
NOUNS	**ADJECTIVES**	**VERBS**	**MISC.**
car	curly	drove	hamster
boat	purple	~~danced~~	dog
roller skate	wet	drank	cat
taxicab	tired	twirled	~~giraffe~~
~~surfboard~~	silly	swam	monkey

"Goodbye!" he said, as he jumped into his _SURFBOARD_ and _DANCED_
    ★   ➡

off with his pet _GIRAFFE_.
    ?

MAD LIBS 😊 JUNIOR
QUICK REVIEW

In case you haven't learned about the parts of speech yet, here is a quick lesson:

A **NOUN** ★ is the name of a person, place, or thing. *Sidewalk, umbrella, bathtub,* and *roller skates* are nouns.

An **ADJECTIVE** 😎 describes a person, place, or thing. *Lumpy, soft, ugly, messy,* and *short* are adjectives.

A **VERB** ➡ is an action word. *Run, jump,* and *swim* are verbs.

MISC. ? can be any word at all. Some examples of a word that could be miscellaneous are: *nose, monkey, five,* and *blue.*

MAD LIBS JUNIOR® is fun to play with friends, but you can also play it by yourself! To begin, look at the story on the page below. When you come to a blank space in the story, look at the symbol that appears underneath. Then find the same symbol on this page and pick a word that appears below the symbol. Put that word in the blank space, and cross out the word, so you don't use it again. Continue doing this throughout the story until you've filled in all the spaces. Finally, read your story aloud and laugh!

THE WORLD'S NAUGHTIEST BUNNY

★ NOUNS	😀 ADJECTIVES	➡ VERBS	? MISC.
banana	crazy	fish	clouds
mitten	shiny	sleep	shirts
phone	silly	giggle	purses
pillow	big	write	houses
folder	stinky	nibble	plants
book	tiny	jump	belts
tree	pretty	walk	pictures
chair	awesome	hug	bowls
roof	slippery	shout	clocks
hat	goofy	smile	peas
pencil	quiet	wiggle	chimneys
dress	funny	frown	balloons

MAD LIBS JUNIOR.
THE WORLD'S NAUGHTIEST BUNNY

Hi! My name is Peter Rabbit. It's _____ to meet you!

I just might be the naughtiest _____ in the world.

I often get into lots of _____! But I'm also a very

_____ bunny, and I have a good _____ .

Let me tell you about my beautiful blue _____ . It's very

_____ because it used to belong to my _____ .

I love to wear it wherever I _____ . And even though I

always wear my jacket, I never wear _____ . My favorite

thing to eat is a nice big _____ . Yummy! If you ask

me, the best place to find juicy _____ is in Thomas

McGregor's _____ . Thomas McGregor thinks he's

_____ , but he's not as _____ as me! I will always

find a way to _____ him!

MAD LIBS JUNIOR® is fun to play with friends, but you can also play it by yourself! To begin, look at the story on the page below. When you come to a blank space in the story, look at the symbol that appears underneath. Then find the same symbol on this page and pick a word that appears below the symbol. Put that word in the blank space, and cross out the word, so you don't use it again. Continue doing this throughout the story until you've filled in all the spaces. Finally, read your story aloud and laugh!

PETER'S BEST FRIEND

★ NOUNS	☺ ADJECTIVES	➔ VERBS	? MISC.
car	mushy	skip	shoes
table	gigantic	climb	water bottles
tape	loud	laugh	sharks
lamp	lovely	drive	scissors
clock	spicy	sit	zippers
ruler	lumpy	waddle	fences
door	dirty	dive	glasses
cup	clean	grow	ears
key	lazy	dance	rainbows
pickle	smooth	sneeze	cameras
cookie	delicious	color	farts
jelly bean	mean	juggle	noodles

MAD LIBS JUNIOR.
PETER'S BEST FRIEND

I'm Peter Rabbit's cousin and best ⭐_____, Benjamin

Bunny. Peter is a ⭐_____, and he acts very

👀_____. I am a lot more 👀_____ and a bit

of a ⭐_____. Peter usually has crazy **?**_____

about what games to ➡_____ and how to steal

?_____ from Thomas McGregor's ⭐_____.

I do my best to talk Peter out of his **?**_____,

but he doesn't usually ➡_____ with my ideas.

But we're family, and families ➡_____ together!

Oh **?**_____! It looks like Peter is planning to ➡_____

into Thomas McGregor's garden. Time for me to try and

➡_____ him!

MAD LIBS JUNIOR® is fun to play with friends, but you can also play it by yourself! To begin, look at the story on the page below. When you come to a blank space in the story, look at the symbol that appears underneath. Then find the same symbol on this page and pick a word that appears below the symbol. Put that word in the blank space, and cross out the word, so you don't use it again. Continue doing this throughout the story until you've filled in all the spaces. Finally, read your story aloud and laugh!

FLOPSY: THE YOUNGEST TRIPLET

★ NOUNS	☺ ADJECTIVES	→ VERBS	? MISC.
snails	fuzzy	knit	president
cucumbers	fizzy	stomp	alligator
donuts	prickly	smell	gorilla
sneakers	bumpy	bounce	skyscraper
windows	awkward	stretch	whale
jackets	boring	tickle	ocean
fairies	scaly	shake	wizard
spiders	disgusting	clean	rattlesnake
trucks	bad	bump	tarantula
turkeys	plain	flip	rainbow
wolves	curly	lick	waterfall
aliens	friendly	swing	lollipop

MAD LIBS JUNIOR.
FLOPSY: THE YOUNGEST TRIPLET

Peter is usually the _____**?** of attention, but he does

have _____☺ sisters. And I'm one of them—Flopsy.

Because Peter is older, he always thinks he's the _____**?**

of the family. Peter is very good at getting into _____⭐,

and my _____⭐ and I don't always go along with

his _____☺ plans. But one time he did convince us

to _____➡ blackberries and _____⭐ at Thomas

McGregor's house. One of the _____⭐ I threw knocked

some sparrows out of a/an _____**?**. Sorry! My sisters and

I kind of _____➡ alike. The best way to identify me is by

my cute _____**?**. My _____**?** used to bother me,

but now I think it makes me look _____☺!

MAD LIBS JUNIOR® is fun to play with friends, but you can also play it by yourself! To begin, look at the story on the page below. When you come to a blank space in the story, look at the symbol that appears underneath. Then find the same symbol on this page and pick a word that appears below the symbol. Put that word in the blank space, and cross out the word, so you don't use it again. Continue doing this throughout the story until you've filled in all the spaces. Finally, read your story aloud and laugh!

MOPSY: SISTERS RULE

★ NOUNS	☺ ADJECTIVES	➡ VERBS	? MISC.
trumpets	dizzy	fly	belly button
flowers	funny	bite	shoe box
computers	bubbly	kiss	sandwich
eggs	painful	burp	unicycle
stars	damp	tickle	mailbox
wishes	scary	juggle	doghouse
chickens	slimy	eat	garbage can
piglets	goofy	polish	file cabinet
pirates	frizzy	snuggle	sailboat
dancers	dark	fix	dungeon
ghosts	gloomy	vacuum	dresser
ponies	slippery	share	castle

I'm Mopsy, another one of Peter's _____ ⭐ . We all

_____ ➡️ Peter, but he can make us a bit _____ 😊

at times! But since we don't have any _____ ⭐ , and

Peter is very _____ 😊 , he is usually the one in charge.

Everyone in the _____ ❓ is good at something, and

I'm really good at sewing. In fact, I sew _____ ⭐ for

everyone. Do you like my yellow _____ ❓ ? I think it's

_____ 😊 . Peter always has to have a blue _____ ❓ .

Flopsy has a _____ 😊 red jacket with a _____ ❓

on it. And Cotton-tail's coat has _____ ⭐ . Shall I sew a

_____ ❓ for you, too?

MAD LIBS JUNIOR® is fun to play with friends, but you can also play it by yourself! To begin, look at the story on the page below. When you come to a blank space in the story, look at the symbol that appears underneath. Then find the same symbol on this page and pick a word that appears below the symbol. Put that word in the blank space, and cross out the word, so you don't use it again. Continue doing this throughout the story until you've filled in all the spaces. Finally, read your story aloud and laugh!

DON'T FORGET ABOUT COTTON-TAIL!

★ NOUNS	☺ ADJECTIVES	→ VERBS	? MISC.
bathrobe	bossy	mop	excuse me
snowball	important	chew	yippee
piano	new	blink	yuck
campfire	early	follow	cool
tooth	different	freeze	really
worm	great	invent	awesome
sink	deadly	scratch	see ya
pizza	greedy	paint	seriously
meatball	itchy	pop	no way
dragon	spiky	scribble	duh
elf	perfect	surprise	super
monster	wicked	mix	what

MAD LIBS JUNIOR.
DON'T FORGET ABOUT COTTON-TAIL!

_____ **?** ! Don't _____ **→** about me—Cotton-tail.

Why is my _____ **★** always last in the list of Peter's

_____ **☺** sisters? Well, everyone might remember Flopsy

and Mopsy's names before mine, but I am just as much of

a/an _____ **☺** _____ **★** as my _____ **☺** brother!

I always have my _____ **★** to the ground, and I join Peter

on his _____ **☺** missions. I am just as good at kicking

around a/an _____ **★** , throwing a/an _____ **★** , and

stealing a/an _____ **★** from Thomas McGregor's garden.

_____ **?** ! I even helped _____ **→** the electric fence

back into Thomas McGregor's house. _____ **?** !

MAD LIBS JUNIOR® is fun to play with friends, but you can also play it by yourself! To begin, look at the story on the page below. When you come to a blank space in the story, look at the symbol that appears underneath. Then find the same symbol on this page and pick a word that appears below the symbol. Put that word in the blank space, and cross out the word, so you don't use it again. Continue doing this throughout the story until you've filled in all the spaces. Finally, read your story aloud and laugh!

QUITE THE PIG

★ NOUNS	☺ ADJECTIVES	→ VERBS	? MISC.
taco	baggy	avoid	french fries
towel	fresh	clip	buttons
candle	hungry	float	puppies
potato	heavy	brush	mirrors
basket	muddy	open	shoelaces
cup	flaky	whistle	marshmallows
tennis ball	droopy	sparkle	flowers
bandage	crowded	drink	boxes
grill	flat	glue	feathers
bridge	jealous	type	dolls
bell	neat	enjoy	pineapples
frog	old	exercise	fireflies

MAD LIBS JUNIOR
QUITE THE PIG

Well, hello there. Let me _____ ➡ myself. My name is

Pigling Bland, and I am the most _____ 😊 pig you've

ever met. Do you _____ ➡ any other pig who wears a

beautiful velvet _____ ⭐ , carries a/an _____ 😊 cane,

and drinks from a/an _____ 😊 gold cup? And don't forget

about my beautiful pocket _____ ⭐ ! You know what they

say—a pig should always _____ ➡ his best. I live with all

my _____ ❓ at the lovely McGregor Manor. Peter might

be a bit _____ 😊 and make _____ ❓ wherever he

goes, but he is a good _____ ⭐ and likes to have parties.

And I love a/an _____ 😊 party! So perhaps you'd like to

come _____ ➡ with us at the manor sometime?

Published in 2018 by Mad Libs, an imprint of Penguin Random House LLC.

MAD LIBS JUNIOR® is fun to play with friends, but you can also play it by yourself! To begin, look at the story on the page below. When you come to a blank space in the story, look at the symbol that appears underneath. Then find the same symbol on this page and pick a word that appears below the symbol. Put that word in the blank space, and cross out the word, so you don't use it again. Continue doing this throughout the story until you've filled in all the spaces. Finally, read your story aloud and laugh!

NEW LIFE IN THE COUNTRY

★ NOUNS	☺ ADJECTIVES	→ VERBS	? MISC.
fireplace	pushy	dream	yee-haw
mustache	lucky	eat	cheers
mop	polite	wave	ugh
pool	tight	wag	gosh
earring	rich	jiggle	darn
bathroom	sleepy	forget	crikey
furnace	soggy	kneel	ahoy
vent	shabby	peep	eureka
barrel	weak	twist	gadzooks
wagon	zany	toast	shazam

MAD LIBS JUNIOR.
NEW LIFE IN THE COUNTRY

Hi! _____ ➡ at us! We're the _____ 😊 little gerbils

who used to run around on a wheel in a/an _____ ⭐ . But

now we're _____ 😊 . _____ ❓ ! When we got on that

_____ ⭐ in London, we weren't sure where we were going.

But thanks to that _____ ⭐ wearing _____ 😊 clothes,

we are now living in the _____ 😊 Lake District. We get

to _____ ➡ in this _____ 😊 house with lots of new

friends, including a prickly _____ ⭐ , a _____ 😊

duck, and a very naughty _____ ⭐ . It's our _____ 😊

new life in the country. _____ ❓ !

MAD LIBS JUNIOR® is fun to play with friends, but you can also play it by yourself! To begin, look at the story on the page below. When you come to a blank space in the story, look at the symbol that appears underneath. Then find the same symbol on this page and pick a word that appears below the symbol. Put that word in the blank space, and cross out the word, so you don't use it again. Continue doing this throughout the story until you've filled in all the spaces. Finally, read your story aloud and laugh!

A REAL CITY MOUSE

★ NOUNS	☺ ADJECTIVES	➜ VERBS	? MISC.
toaster	oily	swallow	pens
painting	messy	draw	rubber bands
mattress	slippery	drill	trays
vase	soft	mow	bricks
jar	hard	wash	candles
shelf	dusty	scrub	statues
table	funny	stir	towels
lamp	awful	push	sleds
dresser	tall	skate	coupons
basket	wicked	dance	cookies
curtain	gentle	buzz	kittens
street	careful	drag	monkeys

Johnny Town-mouse here. Did you ever think you would see

me _____ → the big _____ ★ and head to the

_____ 😊 country? Truthfully, I went because I heard some

_____ ? were throwing the biggest _____ ★ of the

year up at some _____ 😊 manor house. It meant I had

to _____ → on a train and _____ → north. Luckily

for me, I made some new best _____ ? on the way there.

And I met even more _____ ? when I got to the manor

house! Plus, I got to _____ → my friends when they

had to find that _____ 😊 human. I heard that it was all

_____ 😊 in the end, though. They better invite me to the

next _____ ★ they have!

MAD LIBS JUNIOR® is fun to play with friends, but you can also play it by yourself! To begin, look at the story on the page below. When you come to a blank space in the story, look at the symbol that appears underneath. Then find the same symbol on this page and pick a word that appears below the symbol. Put that word in the blank space, and cross out the word, so you don't use it again. Continue doing this throughout the story until you've filled in all the spaces. Finally, read your story aloud and laugh!

A VERY HELPFUL HEDGEHOG

★ NOUNS	😎 ADJECTIVES	➡ VERBS	? MISC.
teapot	cold	exercise	babies
cake	angry	hop	hands
school	flaky	mend	windows
nest	gummy	press	fish
list	pesky	rinse	sticks
flag	playful	tumble	milk
seed	ticklish	wrestle	pockets
caterpillar	phony	twinkle	butterflies
ocean	cozy	yell	boogers
vampire	curly	punch	teeth

MAD LIBS JUNIOR.
A VERY HELPFUL HEDGEHOG

_____ ➡ goodness I'm here! I'm Mrs. Tiggy-winkle,

the _____ 😊 hedgehog who does her very best to keep

Peter and his _____ ? in line. They don't have the best

_____ ? , and I have to _____ ➡ after Peter and his

friends all the time. I guess that makes me a little bit of a/an

_____ ★ to all of them. I _____ ➡ my best to keep

McGregor Manor neat and _____ 😊 . But that's hard to do

when Peter and his friends throw big _____ ? all the time!

I guess that means that I'll have to _____ ➡ even more.

Thank _____ ? I'm around!

MAD LIBS JUNIOR® is fun to play with friends, but you can also play it by yourself! To begin, look at the story on the page below. When you come to a blank space in the story, look at the symbol that appears underneath. Then find the same symbol on this page and pick a word that appears below the symbol. Put that word in the blank space, and cross out the word, so you don't use it again. Continue doing this throughout the story until you've filled in all the spaces. Finally, read your story aloud and laugh!

THE SIMPLE LIFE!

★ NOUNS	☺ ADJECTIVES	➡ VERBS	? MISC.
pancake	sweaty	drop	100,000
collar	drowsy	love	6½
beach ball	sour	fart	1,001
tulip	spicy	climb	0
banana	gross	squish	74
ponytail	lacy	jiggle	46
necklace	hairy	lick	839
toothbrush	wiry	scream	7
tuba	fuzzy	rush	25,000
canoe	ugly	nap	506
Jet Ski	purple	study	99
sand castle	murky	drive	33¼

MAD LIBS ☺ JUNIOR.
THE SIMPLE LIFE!

I don't really have time to stop and _____ ➡, but

it would be _____ ☺ not to _____ ➡ myself.

My name is Thomas McGregor. My great-_____ ★

left me McGregor Manor in his _____ ★. It is a/an

_____ ☺ manor in the _____ ★ District, but it has

been taken over by _____ ? animals who like to run wild!

We've got everything from mice to frogs, including some very

_____ ☺ rabbits. But this _____ ★ is mine now, and

I won't let some _____ ☺ vermin ruin it for me. Plus, there

is a beautiful _____ ★ who lives down the road. If I could,

I would stare at her _____ ? times a day. Oh no! There

goes another _____ ★! I'll _____ ➡ them, if it's the

last thing I do!

MAD LIBS JUNIOR® is fun to play with friends, but you can also play it by yourself! To begin, look at the story on the page below. When you come to a blank space in the story, look at the symbol that appears underneath. Then find the same symbol on this page and pick a word that appears below the symbol. Put that word in the blank space, and cross out the word, so you don't use it again. Continue doing this throughout the story until you've filled in all the spaces. Finally, read your story aloud and laugh!

SAVE THE BUNNIES!

★ NOUNS	☺ ADJECTIVES	➜ VERBS	? MISC.
wallet	flashy	drive	hornets
strawberry	bubbly	wink	robots
waffle	wavy	cough	goldfish
noodle	lumpy	sparkle	diamonds
movie	hasty	ask	kitchens
egg	wobbly	break	cards
marker	rusty	bomb	Hula Hoops
machine	busy	bake	lockers
backyard	grimy	freeze	baseballs
beard	fussy	hunt	camels
bed	alert	lift	bricks
mall	white	open	bells

MAD LIBS JUNIOR
SAVE THE BUNNIES!

I'm Bea, and unlike the McGregors, I am a/an _____ 👓

human. I am so _____ 😊 that I am around to

_____ ➡ Peter and his _____ ❓ . _____ 👓

Mr. McGregor did his best to _____ ➡ the animals

that lived in his _____ ⭐ , but those _____ 👓

animals usually got away—except for Peter's _____ ⭐ .

(_____ 😊 bunny—he ended up in a/an _____ ⭐ !)

Old Mr. McGregor's _____ 😊 -nephew is a bit more

_____ 😊 and has more tricks up his _____ ⭐ . Well,

it seems to be _____ 😊 at the moment, so I may see if I

have time to hang up some of my _____ ❓ .

MAD LIBS JUNIOR® is fun to play with friends, but you can also play it by yourself! To begin, look at the story on the page below. When you come to a blank space in the story, look at the symbol that appears underneath. Then find the same symbol on this page and pick a word that appears below the symbol. Put that word in the blank space, and cross out the word, so you don't use it again. Continue doing this throughout the story until you've filled in all the spaces. Finally, read your story aloud and laugh!

A VISIT TO MCGREGOR MANOR

★ NOUNS	☺ ADJECTIVES	➡ VERBS	? MISC.
newspaper	wrong	measure	spoons
spatula	green	flick	batteries
firecracker	cracked	wipe	photos
carpet	scrawny	swim	dice
cap	skinny	lift	cheese
star	shimmery	tie	aprons
smile	tight	rush	clouds
bucket	cozy	scribble	notepads
shoelace	loose	spin	buses
moon	hollow	snarl	rings
field	jolly	lock	pants
band	grand	overflow	chalk

MAD LIBS ☺ JUNIOR.
A VISIT TO MCGREGOR MANOR

Down a _____ country road in the beautiful

English _____ is the _____ McGregor

Manor. It is made from _____ stone and lots of

_____ that let in the warm English _____.

It is surrounded by _____, green woods that are

home to lots of _____. (That is, when they are

not trying to _____ in the manor!) The manor has

been in the McGregor _____ for generations. It was

_____ for a while, but then Thomas McGregor moved

in and a lot of _____ changed! Thomas won't let any of

those _____ animals _____ in the house with

him, but the delicious _____ is another matter!

MAD LIBS JUNIOR® is fun to play with friends, but you can also play it by yourself! To begin, look at the story on the page below. When you come to a blank space in the story, look at the symbol that appears underneath. Then find the same symbol on this page and pick a word that appears below the symbol. Put that word in the blank space, and cross out the word, so you don't use it again. Continue doing this throughout the story until you've filled in all the spaces. Finally, read your story aloud and laugh!

GARDEN MENU

★ NOUNS	☺ ADJECTIVES	➡ VERBS	? MISC.
T-shirt	plump	name	silver
chart	teeny	ignore	pink
policeman	slippery	point	polka-dotted
ladder	foolish	knock	rainbow
car	stiff	enjoy	gold
mat	cheerful	spin	white
friend	tall	print	black
candy bar	dull	chat	bronze
straw	pointy	slip	purple
arrow	grumpy	frown	beige
patch	hot	burp	aqua
enemy	magical	fall	brown

MAD LIBS JUNIOR.
GARDEN MENU

The part of _____ McGregor Manor that is of most

interest to Peter and his _____ friends is the big

_____. It is full of all kinds of _____ things to

⭐ _____ , such as:

Tasty _____ corn
?

Crunchy _____ carrots
?

_____ juicy tomatoes

Yummy _____-berries
?

Big, _____ eggplants

Beautiful _____-flowers
⭐

Bright _____ pumpkins
?

_____ green lettuce

And Peter's favorite—_____ _____ radishes!
?

MAD LIBS JUNIOR® is fun to play with friends, but you can also play it by yourself! To begin, look at the story on the page below. When you come to a blank space in the story, look at the symbol that appears underneath. Then find the same symbol on this page and pick a word that appears below the symbol. Put that word in the blank space, and cross out the word, so you don't use it again. Continue doing this throughout the story until you've filled in all the spaces. Finally, read your story aloud and laugh!

A TRIP TO THE BIG CITY

★ NOUNS	☺ ADJECTIVES	→ VERBS	? MISC.
mirror	cramped	fly	combs
hairbrush	kooky	drain	sinks
hill	warm	clap	seat belts
number	massive	bowl	legs
blackboard	pink	scoot	whiskers
bun	freaky	hum	sponges
dart	prickly	twirl	pineapples
clock	puffy	twist	pebbles
handbag	light	crash	scarves
dumpling	refreshing	hide	olives

MAD LIBS 😊 JUNIOR.
A TRIP TO THE BIG CITY

Thomas McGregor is leaving the _____ ⭐ and

heading back to London. He's had enough of those pesky

_____ **?** and their _____ 😊 tricks! Peter knows that

Bea loves Thomas, and she wants Thomas to _____ ➡

at McGregor Manor. So, Peter and Benjamin _____ ➡

on a _____ ⭐ and go after him. Luckily for them,

the _____ 😊 Johnny Town-mouse is there to help them.

Johnny guides Peter and Benjamin through the city—on

_____ **?** , on _____ **?** , on a _____ ⭐ ,

and right past the famous landmark _____ 😊 Ben! Their

_____ 😊 trip ends where Thomas works—at Harrods, the

_____ 😊 department store where anything is possible.

MAD LIBS JUNIOR® is fun to play with friends, but you can also play it by yourself! To begin, look at the story on the page below. When you come to a blank space in the story, look at the symbol that appears underneath. Then find the same symbol on this page and pick a word that appears below the symbol. Put that word in the blank space, and cross out the word, so you don't use it again. Continue doing this throughout the story until you've filled in all the spaces. Finally, read your story aloud and laugh!

VEGETABLE FIREWORKS

★ NOUNS	☺ ADJECTIVES	➡ VERBS	? MISC.
fern	proud	chop	sodas
lip	fearless	chomp	puddles
blimp	whiny	listen	magazines
squirrel	lively	shop	men
cake	loose	dance	ballerinas
teacher	curvy	doodle	nickels
apple	filthy	glue	cats
label	flat	fib	boxes
party	rainy	swim	glasses
robin	rotten	decide	pins
envelope	crooked	taste	mailboxes
pumpkin	tiny	skate	monkeys

Most country houses are _____ places. However, that's

not the case when Peter and all his _____ **?** are around!

They will do whatever it takes to _____ **➡** McGregor

Manor as their own. That means they will have to fight

_____ **★** and _____ **★** with Thomas McGregor. And

what will they use? Why, _____ **?** of course! Peter and his

friends _____ **➡** themselves with _____ plums,

purple _____ **?** , _____ lettuce, and whatever else

they can _____ **➡** from the garden. *Boom! Bang! Splat!*

MAD LIBS JUNIOR® is fun to play with friends, but you can also play it by yourself! To begin, look at the story on the page below. When you come to a blank space in the story, look at the symbol that appears underneath. Then find the same symbol on this page and pick a word that appears below the symbol. Put that word in the blank space, and cross out the word, so you don't use it again. Continue doing this throughout the story until you've filled in all the spaces. Finally, read your story aloud and laugh!

FAMILY FOREVER

★ NOUNS	☺ ADJECTIVES	➡ VERBS	? MISC.
mushroom	shiny	vibrate	sentences
reindeer	square	turn	alligators
chicken	narrow	tickle	skates
fish	steep	hug	logs
potato	wide	lick	peas
clock	gigantic	cut	cows
calf	woolly	color	dots
book	selfish	exercise	tiles
letter	rich	pat	tools
dinosaur	quiet	call	toads

MAD LIBS JUNIOR.
FAMILY FOREVER

Like most _____**?**_____, Peter and his _____ⓘ sisters

don't always get along, and they _____➡️ from time to

time. But they also _____➡️ each other very much

and will always have each other's _____**?** in times of

need. Peter is very _____ⓘ about his _____**?** .

He has taught them how to be lookouts, how to _____➡️

pebbles and _____**?** , and how not to get caught by the

_____ⓘ McGregors. Of course, those are the lessons

that your big _____⭐ will teach you when he's the world's

naughtiest _____⭐!

Published in 2018 by Mad Libs, an imprint of Penguin Random House LLC.

MAD LIBS JUNIOR® is fun to play with friends, but you can also play it by yourself! To begin, look at the story on the page below. When you come to a blank space in the story, look at the symbol that appears underneath. Then find the same symbol on this page and pick a word that appears below the symbol. Put that word in the blank space, and cross out the word, so you don't use it again. Continue doing this throughout the story until you've filled in all the spaces. Finally, read your story aloud and laugh!

ABSOLUTELY ELECTRIC!

★ NOUNS	☺ ADJECTIVES	→ VERBS	? MISC.
duck	cranky	draw	seaweed
pretzel	golden	memorize	posters
elf	confused	juggle	chimneys
turkey	patient	explode	ashes
building	sticky	jab	paper clips
Ferris wheel	goofy	snort	helicopters
hot dog	fancy	pinch	poodles
sandwich	greasy	wrestle	mothballs
crab	funky	sniff	yo-yos
snail	loopy	gargle	sandals

MAD LIBS JUNIOR
ABSOLUTELY ELECTRIC!

Old Mr. McGregor used a wooden _____ ★ to keep the

_____ ? out of his garden, but his _____ 🙂-nephew

decided that he needed something new and _____ 🙂 to

do the job. And that something is an electric _____ ★.

(That'll show those pesky _____ ?!) But Peter and his

friends are very _____ 🙂, and they _____ ➡ the

electric _____ ★ into McGregor Manor. So rather than

Thomas zapping the _____ ?, the animals _____ ➡

Thomas! *Zap!* That should _____ ➡ it. The garden belongs

to the _____ ? again!

MAD LIBS JUNIOR® is fun to play with friends, but you can also play it by yourself! To begin, look at the story on the page below. When you come to a blank space in the story, look at the symbol that appears underneath. Then find the same symbol on this page and pick a word that appears below the symbol. Put that word in the blank space, and cross out the word, so you don't use it again. Continue doing this throughout the story until you've filled in all the spaces. Finally, read your story aloud and laugh!

PETER'S PARENTS

★ NOUNS	☺ ADJECTIVES	➡ VERBS	? MISC.
cheeseburger	plain	laugh	bananas
squid	nifty	hammer	onions
toilet	light	buy	sawdust
pancake	upside-down	burp	sweatshirts
boot	oily	feed	sardines
sock	excellent	water	belly buttons
baseball	tasty	shoot	flamingos
snowflake	rubbery	trickle	clowns
suitcase	silver	swing	zebras
frying pan	slimy	clap	sausages

Sadly, Peter's parents are no longer around, but he carries them

in his _____ ★. Peter's father taught him how to be

_____ ☺ and naughty, and Peter's mother taught him how

to be caring and _____ ☺. They both continue to speak

to Peter and _____ → him lessons—lessons about his

_____ ★, family, _____ ?, and love. And although

Peter is still a very _____ ☺ rabbit, his parents are very

proud of him.

MAD LIBS JUNIOR® is fun to play with friends, but you can also play it by yourself! To begin, look at the story on the page below. When you come to a blank space in the story, look at the symbol that appears underneath. Then find the same symbol on this page and pick a word that appears below the symbol. Put that word in the blank space, and cross out the word, so you don't use it again. Continue doing this throughout the story until you've filled in all the spaces. Finally, read your story aloud and laugh!

A LESSON IN RABBITS

★ NOUNS	😀 ADJECTIVES	➡ VERBS	? MISC.
bedroom	slick	whistle	closets
garage	crunchy	test	submarines
spaceship	lazy	wrestle	garbage cans
office	faded	explore	drawers
parking lot	thick	park	pencil cases
shipyard	thin	drive	refrigerators
apartment	glossy	win	stoves
kitchen	smelly	fish	canoes
theater	awful	squeeze	restaurants
doghouse	tiny	cook	cans

MAD LIBS JUNIOR.
A LESSON IN RABBITS

Peter, his sisters, and his _____★_____ Benjamin are all

_____👦_____ rabbits. Rabbits are small _____❓_____ found

in several places around the _____★_____. Peter and his family

make their _____★_____ in the Lake District in England.

Rabbit habitats include _____❓_____, woods, forests,

grasslands, _____❓_____, and _____👦_____-lands. But Peter and

his family are special because they _____➡_____ in McGregor

Manor—not a place where you'd usually _____➡_____ rabbits!

Rabbits are most _____👦_____ at dawn and at dusk. Peter, on

the other hand, never sits still, no matter the time of day!

MAD LIBS JUNIOR® is fun to play with friends, but you can also play it by yourself! To begin, look at the story on the page below. When you come to a blank space in the story, look at the symbol that appears underneath. Then find the same symbol on this page and pick a word that appears below the symbol. Put that word in the blank space, and cross out the word, so you don't use it again. Continue doing this throughout the story until you've filled in all the spaces. Finally, read your story aloud and laugh!

THE LOVELY LAKE DISTRICT

★ NOUNS	☺ ADJECTIVES	➡ VERBS	? MISC.
tin can	salty	yell	lightbulbs
nut	rocky	sing	worms
stapler	fresh	melt	cherries
butter	old	scratch	clouds
jelly	orange	burp	lizards
bubble gum	chewy	lick	peanuts
river	nerdy	study	giants
teapot	blue	flip	dolphins
telephone	chubby	sew	straws
toothbrush	horrible	hide	watermelons
iceberg	creepy	spit	dump trucks
hamburger	strange	fart	toenails

Peter, his family, and his _____ **?** live in the _____ 😊

Lake District. It is a mountainous _____ ★ located

in northwest England that is famous for its lakes, forests,

_____ **?** —and rabbits. There are many meadows full

of _____ **?** —and don't forget the rabbits. The sunrises

and _____ **?** are _____ 😊 —just like the rabbits!

Many writers and _____ **?** have lived in the _____ **?** .

The beauty of the area inspired them to _____ → poems,

books—and, of course, lots of stories about _____ 😊 rabbits!

MAD LIBS JUNIOR® is fun to play with friends, but you can also play it by yourself! To begin, look at the story on the page below. When you come to a blank space in the story, look at the symbol that appears underneath. Then find the same symbol on this page and pick a word that appears below the symbol. Put that word in the blank space, and cross out the word, so you don't use it again. Continue doing this throughout the story until you've filled in all the spaces. Finally, read your story aloud and laugh!

HAPPILY EVER AFTER?

★ NOUNS	☺ ADJECTIVES	→ VERBS	? MISC.
clam	lucky	grab	lobsters
lizard	angry	pinch	bananas
star	super	fold	forks
dish	black	march	hangers
bicycle	fuzzy	stir	coconuts
compass	straight	lean	posters
belt	leafy	laugh	marbles
carpet	loud	barf	boogers
tire	damp	dance	mops
bean	short	jump	snowballs

MAD LIBS 😊 JUNIOR.
HAPPILY EVER AFTER?

In a/an _____ 😊 storage room, somewhere in London:

Peter: Thomas, you must _____ ➡ back to McGregor

_____ ★ . Bea is going to leave!

Thomas: _____ ? ! She can't do that!

Peter: I _____ ➡ ! That's why you have to stop her.

I'm sorry I tried to _____ ➡ you, and that I put _____ ?

on your head, and that I rubbed my _____ ★ on your

toothbrush. But you have to stop her!

Thomas: How do I know that this isn't a _____ ★ ?

Peter: You just have to trust me.

Thomas: I _____ ➡ Bea so much.

Peter: So do I.

Thomas: Well, then let's _____ ➡ !